# Collins

## Grammar, Punctuation and Vocabulary Progress Tests

Year 4/P5

Author:
**Abigail Steel**

Series editor:
**Stephanie Austwick**

William Collins' dream of knowledge for all began with the publication of his first book in 1819. A self-educated mill worker, he not only enriched millions of lives, but also founded a flourishing publishing house. Today, staying true to this spirit, Collins books are packed with inspiration, innovation and practical expertise. They place you at the centre of a world of possibility and give you exactly what you need to explore it.

Collins. Freedom to teach.

Published by Collins
An imprint of HarperCollins*Publishers*
The News Building
1 London Bridge Street
London SE1 9GF

Browse the complete Collins catalogue at www.collins.co.uk

© HarperCollins*Publishers* Limited 2019

10 9 8 7 6 5 4 3 2 1

ISBN 978-0-00-833364-5

All rights reserved. No part of this publication may be reproduced, stored in a retrieval system, or transmitted in any form by any means, electronic, mechanical, photocopying, recording or otherwise, without the prior written permission of the Publisher or a licence permitting restricted copying in the United Kingdom issued by the Copyright Licensing Agency Ltd., Barnard's Inn, 86 Fetter Lane, London, EC4A 1EN.

British Library Cataloguing in Publication Data. A catalogue record for this publication is available from the British Library.

Author: Abigail Steel

Series Editor: Stephanie Austwick

Publisher: Katie Sergeant

Product Manager: Sarah Thomas

Content Editor: Holly Woolnough

Copyeditor and proofreader: Tanya Solomons

Reviewer: Rachel Clarke

Internal design and typesetting: Hugh Hillyard-Parker

Cover designers: The Big Mountain Design and Ken Vail Graphic Design

Production Controller: Katharine Willard

# Contents

How to use this book · 4

Year 4 Curriculum map: Yearly overview · 6

**Year 4/P5 Half Termly Tests**
Autumn Half Term 1 · 7
Autumn Half Term 2 · 16
Spring Half Term 1 · 24
Spring Half Term 2 · 33
Summer Half Term 1 · 41
Summer Half Term 2 · 50

**Mark schemes**
Autumn Half Term 1 · 59
Autumn Half Term 2 · 61
Spring Half Term 1 · 63
Spring Half Term 2 · 65
Summer Half Term 1 · 67
Summer Half Term 2 · 69

Record sheet · 71

# How to use this book

## Introduction

Collins *Grammar, Punctuation and Vocabulary Progress Tests* have been designed to give you a consistent whole-school approach to teaching and assessing grammar, punctuation and vocabulary. Each photocopiable book covers the required vocabulary, grammar and punctuation objectives from the English National Curriculum statutory guidance and vocabulary, grammar and punctuation appendix. For teachers in Scotland, the books can offer guidance and structure that is not provided in the Curriculum for Excellence Experiences and Outcomes or Benchmarks.

Revision of previous years' work is also included, where appropriate, to ensure children are building their skills to become confident and secure users of grammar, punctuation and vocabulary. As standalone tests, independent of any teaching and learning scheme, the Collins *Grammar, Punctuation and Vocabulary Progress Tests* provide a structured way to assess progress in grammar, punctuation and vocabulary, to help you identify areas for development, and to provide evidence towards expectations for each year group.

## Building confidence and understanding

At the end of Key Stage 1 and Key Stage 2, children are assessed on their understanding of grammar, punctuation and vocabulary. This is done through teacher assessment of children's writing, through the grammar, punctuation and vocabulary SAT in KS2 and through the optional SAT in KS1. Collins *Grammar, Punctuation and Vocabulary Progress Tests* have been designed to help children recognise grammatical features whilst building familiarity with the format, language and style of the SATs. Through regular use of the Collins *Grammar, Punctuation and Vocabulary Progress Tests* children should develop and practise the necessary skills to complete the national tests confidently and proficiently.

The Collins *Grammar, Punctuation and Vocabulary Progress Tests* are written so that new grammatical content is presented in a variety of ways with increasing challenge over the tests in the book. Previous learning is also addressed in Years 2 – 6 with questions that ask children to recall grammar, punctuation and vocabulary learned in previous year groups.

## How to use this book

In this book, you will find six photocopiable half-termly tests, written to replicate the format of the SATs with space for children to write their answers. You will also find a Curriculum Map on page 6 indicating the aspects of the Content Domain covered in each test and across the year group. These have been cross-referenced with the appropriate age-related statements from the National Curriculum. In KS2, each test should take 35 – 45 minutes to complete and in KS1 each test should take approximately 20 minutes. KS1 teachers may prefer to administer each test in two halves of 10 minutes each, and in Year 1 read each question to children.

To help you mark the tests, you will find mark schemes that include the number of marks to be awarded, model answers and a reference to the elements of the Content Domain covered by each question.

## Test demand

The tests have been written to ensure smooth progression in children's understanding of grammar, punctuation and vocabulary within the book and across the rest of the books in the series. Each test builds on those before it so that children are guided towards the expectations of the SATs at the end of KS1 and KS2.

Year 4: How to use this book

| Year group | Number of marks per test |
|---|---|
| 1 | 20 |
| 2 | 20 |
| 3 | 30 |
| 4 | 30 |
| 5 | 40 |
| 6 | 50 |

## Performance thresholds

The table below provides guidance for assessing how children perform in the tests. Most children should achieve scores at or above the expected standard with some children working at greater depth and exceeding expectations for their year group. Whilst these threshold bands do not represent standardised scores, as in the end of key stage SATs, they will give an indication of how children are performing against the expected standard for their year group.

| Year group | Working towards | Expected standard | Greater depth |
|---|---|---|---|
| 1 | 9 marks or below | 10–16 marks | 17–20 marks |
| 2 | 9 marks or below | 10–16 marks | 17–20 marks |
| 3 | 14 marks or below | 15–25 marks | 26–30 marks |
| 4 | 14 marks or below | 15–25 marks | 26–30 marks |
| 5 | 18 marks or below | 19–33 marks | 34–40 marks |
| 6 | 23 marks or below | 24–42 marks | 43–50 marks |

## Tracking progress

A record sheet is provided to help you illustrate to children the areas in which they have performed well and where they need to develop. A spreadsheet tracker is also provided via
**collins.co.uk/assessment/downloads** which enables you to identify whole-class patterns of attainment. This can then be used to inform your next teaching and learning steps.

## Editable download

All the files are available in Word and PDF format for you to edit if you wish. Go to
**collins.co.uk/assessment/downloads** to find instructions on how to download. The files are password protected and the password clue is included on the website. You will need to use the clue to locate the password in your book. You can use these editable files to help you meet the specific needs of your class, whether that be by increasing or decreasing the challenge, by reducing the number of questions, by providing more space for answers or increasing the size of text as required for specific children.

© HarperCollinsPublishers Ltd 2019

# Year 4 Curriculum map: Yearly overview

| National Curriculum objective (Year 4) | Content domain | Autumn Test 1 | Autumn Test 2 | Spring Test 1 | Spring Test 2 | Summer Test 1 | Summer Test 2 |
|---|---|---|---|---|---|---|---|
| **WORD** | | | | | | | |
| The grammatical difference between plural and possessive –s | G5 | ● | ● | | | | ● |
| Standard English forms for verb inflections instead of local spoken forms [for example, *we were* instead of *we was*, or *I did* instead of *I done*] | G7 | | | ● | | ● | ● |
| **SENTENCE** | | | | | | | |
| Noun phrases expanded by the addition of modifying adjectives – *the old tree* | G3 | ● | | ● | | ● | ● |
| Noun phrases expanded by the addition of modifying nouns – *the oak tree* | G3 | | ● | ● | ● | ● | ● |
| Noun phrases expanded by the addition of modifying preposition phrases – *the tree by the gate* | G3 | | | ● | ● | | ● |
| Fronted adverbials [for example, *Later that day, I heard the bad news.*] | G1 | ● | | ● | | ● | ● |
| **TEXT** | | | | | | | |
| Appropriate choice of pronoun or noun within and across sentences to aid cohesion and avoid repetition. | G1 | | | ● | ● | ● | ● |
| **PUNCTUATION** | | | | | | | |
| Use of inverted commas and other punctuation to indicate direct speech [for example, a comma after the reporting clause; end punctuation within inverted commas] | G5 | ● | ● | ● | ● | ● | ● |
| Apostrophes to mark plural possession [for example, *the boys' table*] | G5 | | ● | | ● | | ● |
| Use of commas after fronted adverbials. | G5 | ● | | ● | | ● | ● |

Content Domain Key
G1: Grammatical terms / word clauses
G2: Functions of sentences
G3: Combining words, phrases and clauses
G4: Verb forms, tenses and consistency
G5: Punctuation
G6: Vocabulary
G7: Standard English and formality

# Autumn Half Term 1

**1** Circle all the **determiners** in the sentence below.

We found an old tool box and a lawnmower inside the wooden shed.

1 mark

**2** Tick the **conjunction** in the sentence below.

Tick **one**.

I'm going for a bike ride when the blustery wind calms down.

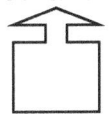   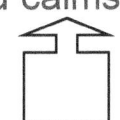

1 mark

**3** Tick **one** box in each row to show whether the underlined word is an **adjective** or an **adverb**.

| Sentence | Adjective | Adverb |
| --- | --- | --- |
| Imogen had a <u>colourful</u> kite. | | |
| She took her kite <u>outside</u>. | | |
| The wind <u>swiftly</u> lifted the kite into the sky. | | |

2 marks

**4** Tick all the sentences that contain a **preposition**.

Tino is below Pete on the list. ☐

The park is beyond the school field. ☐

Eva is ahead of Fran in the race. ☐

Jan closed the door but was still cold. ☐

1 mark

**5** Which sentence is written in the **present perfect**?

Tick **one**.

He has gone home. ☐

He is at home. ☐

He was at home. ☐

He will be at home. ☐

1 mark

**6** Add **inverted commas** to the sentence below to show what Andrew is saying.

Andrew squealed, I am excited about running in the relay race.

1 mark

**7** Tick **one** box in each row to show whether the underlined noun is **singular** or **plural**.

| Sentence | Singular | Plural |
| --- | --- | --- |
| Here are the <u>cats'</u> bowls. | | |
| I have the <u>girl's</u> books. | | |
| These are the <u>boys'</u> shoes. | | |

2 marks

**8** Underline the **noun phrase** in the sentence below.

We watched the brand new action movie.

1 mark

**9** Tick the correct option to complete the sentence below.

_____, we danced at the disco.

Tick **one**.

We wore sparkly t-shirts ☐

The lights shone ☐

Later that evening ☐

I spoke to John ☐

1 mark

**10** Add **inverted commas** to the sentence below to show what Natasha is saying.

Natasha asked, Do you want a sandwich for your lunch today?

1 mark

**11** Which sentence is punctuated correctly?

Tick **one**.

Immediately after school we went, fishing. ☐

Immediately, after school we went fishing. ☐

Immediately after, school we went fishing. ☐

Immediately after school, we went fishing. ☐

1 mark

**12** Choose the correct word to complete each sentence. Write the word on the line.

I saw _____ butterfly sitting on a flower.
    ↓
  [ a / an ]

Grandpa was fetching _____ spade and some gloves.
           ↓
         [ a / an ]

We stayed in the garden for _____ hour before teatime.
              ↓
            [ a / an ]

1 mark

**13** Circle all the **conjunctions** in the sentences below.

Once Dean arrived at the station, he raced to the platform.

He was glad he had run since the train pulled up straight away.

1 mark

**14** Circle the **adverb** in the sentence below.

The postman usually leaves any parcels in our shed if we aren't at home.

*1 mark*

**15** Tick the correct option to complete the sentence below.

There is a carton of orange juice _____ the fridge.

Tick **one**.

| | |
|---|---|
| under | ☐ |
| in | ☐ |
| at | ☐ |
| down | ☐ |

*1 mark*

**16** Which option completes the sentence in the **present perfect**?

Eleanor _____ a fantastic new book.

Tick **one**.

| | |
|---|---|
| will read | ☐ |
| is reading | ☐ |
| has read | ☐ |
| was reading | ☐ |

*1 mark*

**17** Which option uses **inverted commas** correctly?

Tick **one**.

Grandmother asked, "Do you have a tent?" ☐

Grandmother "asked, Do you have a tent?" ☐

"Grandmother asked, Do you have a tent?" ☐

Grandmother asked, "Do you have a tent"? ☐

1 mark

**18** Which sentence uses an **apostrophe** correctly?

Tick **one**.

The childrens toys' were scattered on the floor. ☐

The childrens toy's were scattered on the floor. ☐

The children's toys were scattered on the floor. ☐

The childrens' toys were scattered on the floor. ☐

1 mark

**19** Write an appropriate **adjective** in the box to expand the noun phrase in the sentence.

Anita looked at the ☐ swimming pool.

1 mark

**20** Tick the option that shows how the underlined words in the sentence below are used.

<u>In the distance</u>, Jamal could hear a rumbling noise.

Tick **one**.

as a main clause ☐

as a fronted adverbial ☐

as a subordinate clause ☐

as a noun phrase ☐

1 mark

**21** Add **inverted commas** to the sentence below to show what Kira is saying.

Kira explained, We climbed to the top of the mountain!

1 mark

**22** Tick **one** box to show where the comma following the **fronted adverbial** should go.

Tick **one**.

As quick as a flash the rabbit disappeared into a hole.
  ↑      ↑         ↑              ↑
  ☐      ☐         ☐              ☐

1 mark

**23** Complete the sentence below by writing the **conjunctions** from the box in the correct places. Use each conjunction only once.

| but and or |
|---|

You can go outside _____ play cricket _____ basketball,

_____ you mustn't go on the wet grass.

1 mark

**24** Which **word class** is the underlined word in the sentence below?

The museum has dinosaur skeletons <u>downstairs</u>.

Tick **one**.

| conjunction | ☐ |
| adverb | ☐ |
| verb | ☐ |
| determiner | ☐ |

1 mark

**25** Circle the **preposition** in the sentence below.

There is a huge hairy spider under the table.

1 mark

**26** Which option uses **inverted commas** correctly?

Tick **one**.

"Amit asked, Shall we have a barbecue today?" ☐

Amit asked, "Shall we have a barbecue today"? ☐

Amit asked, Shall we have a "barbecue today?" ☐

Amit asked, "Shall we have a barbecue today?" ☐

1 mark

**27** Complete the sentence with an appropriate **fronted adverbial**.

_____, the thunder and lightning began.

1 mark

**28** Tick the correct option to complete the sentence below.

All of my _____ families will be watching the show.

Tick **one**.

friends ☐

friends' ☐

friend's ☐

friends's ☐

1 mark

Total: _____ /30

Year 4: Autumn Half Term Test 2

| Name: | Year: | Date: |

# Autumn Half Term 2

**1** Tick the sentence that is correct.

Tick **one**.

The cats' tails are long and fluffy. ☐

The cat's tails are long and fluffy. ☐

The cats tail's are long and fluffy. ☐

The cats tails' are long and fluffy. ☐

1 mark

**2** Tick **one** box in each row to show whether the underlined word is an **adjective** or a **noun**.

| Sentence | Adjective | Noun |
|---|---|---|
| We waited by the oak tree. | | |
| I saw a hairy spider. | | |
| My mum is a famous artist. | | |

2 marks

**3** Tick **two** boxes to show the correct places for **inverted commas** in the sentence below.

Tick **two**.

☐        ☐ ☐     ☐

Can we go to the beach today, Dad? asked Helen.

1 mark

**4** Tick **one** box in each row to show whether the underlined noun is **singular** or **plural**.

| Sentence | Singular | Plural |
| --- | --- | --- |
| The <u>girls'</u> bus has arrived at the bus stop. | | |
| Did you see the <u>rocket's</u> boosters? | | |
| <u>Val's</u> hats are in the cupboard. | | |

2 marks

**5** Tick the sentence that is correct.

Tick **one**.

The fox'es den is near the old tree. ☐

The foxe's den is near the old tree. ☐

The foxes' den is near the old tree. ☐

The foxes den is near the old tree. ☐

1 mark

**6** Circle the word in the passage that contains an **apostrophe** for **possession**.

Rubina doesn't know if she's going to Rebecca's party yet.

1 mark

**7** Tick **two** boxes to show which words in the sentence below are **nouns**.

Tick **two**.

We ate chicken soup for dinner yesterday.
   ⇧        ⇧           ⇧          ⇧

1 mark

**8** Tick **one** box in each row to show whether the underlined noun is **singular** or **plural**.

| Sentence | Singular | Plural |
| --- | --- | --- |
| The <u>eagle's</u> nest is high up on the rocks. | | |
| The <u>volcanoes'</u> craters formed many years ago. | | |
| The <u>boys'</u> cinema tickets are in my pocket. | | |

2 marks

**9** Tick all the sentences that show **plural possession**.

Put water in the puppies' bowls please. ☐

Gwen's friends are coming for tea. ☐

The three dogs' leads became tangled. ☐

The postman's bag is full of letters. ☐

1 mark

**10** Add **inverted commas** to the sentence below to show what Hikmat is saying.

Hikmat moaned, I would prefer to have chips for dinner.

1 mark

**11** Underline the **noun phrase** in the sentence below.

The blue china tea cup was broken.

1 mark

**12** Circle the word in the passage below that contains an **apostrophe** for **possession**.

Max has a train set but it doesn't work. He's going to show it to his grandpa. Max's grandpa is good at fixing things.

1 mark

**13** Add **inverted commas** to the sentence below to show what David is saying.

Please wipe your shoes on the mat when you enter the house, said David.

1 mark

**14** Tick **one** box in each row to show whether the underlined noun is **singular** or **plural**.

| Sentence | Singular | Plural |
| --- | --- | --- |
| The <u>families'</u> cars were parked along the street. | | |
| The <u>parents'</u> evening is on Tuesday. | | |
| The <u>woman's</u> scarf is on the chair. | | |

2 marks

**15** Which sentence uses an **apostrophe** correctly?

Tick **one**.

Last Aprils' rainfall was shockingly low. ☐

The childrens' bookshop is closed on Mondays. ☐

My sisters' toy box has a broken lid. ☐

Garys' garage was full of moving boxes. ☐

1 mark

**16** What is the grammatical term for the underlined part of the sentence?

<u>Our heavy old vacuum cleaner</u> sits in the cupboard.

Tick **one**.

a main clause ☐

a fronted adverbial ☐

a noun phrase ☐

a subordinate clause ☐

1 mark

**17** Write an **apostrophe** in the correct place in the sentence below.

The class's performance was great.

1 mark

**18** Which option uses **inverted commas** correctly?

Tick **one**.

Shall we watch the "cricket match?" asked Dev. ☐

"Shall we watch the cricket match"? asked Dev. ☐

"Shall we watch the cricket match? asked Dev." ☐

"Shall we watch the cricket match?" asked Dev. ☐

1 mark

**19** Tick all the sentences that show **plural possession**.

Taylor's parcel arrived today. ☐

The boys' games are brand new. ☐

The tree is full of birds' nests. ☐

Amal's brother's puppy is at the vets. ☐

1 mark

**20** Underline the **noun phrase** in the sentence below.

I am opening a Young Savers bank account today.

1 mark

**21** Which sentence uses an **apostrophe** correctly?

Tick **one**.

Giraffe's necks are very long. ☐

Giraffes' necks are very long. ☐

Giraffes neck's are very long. ☐

Giraffes necks' are very long. ☐

1 mark

**22** Write a **noun phrase** containing at least three words to complete the sentence below.
Remember to punctuate your answer correctly.

I climbed over _____.

1 mark

**23** What is the grammatical term for the underlined part of the sentence below?

<u>The flashing disco lights</u> made the room sparkle.

Tick **one**.

a noun phrase ☐

a main clause ☐

a fronted adverbial ☐

a subordinate clause ☐

1 mark

**24** Explain how the position of the **apostrophe** changes the meaning of the second sentence.

1) The girl's bags were on the bus.

2) The girls' bags were on the bus.

_____

_____

1 mark

**25** Write an appropriate **noun** in the box to expand the noun phrase in the sentence.

We went to the ⬚ shop.

1 mark

**26** Tick all the sentences that show **plural possession**.

I tripped over my brothers' trainers. ☐

The lady's umbrella is soaking wet. ☐

Julia's mum's friend is walking down the path. ☐

The children's toys are in the basket. ☐

1 mark

Total: _____ /30

Year 4: Spring Half Term Test 1

| Name: | Year: | Date: |

# Spring Half Term 1

**1** Which sentence is written in **Standard English**?

Tick **one**.

I went to the museum with my class. ☐

I been to the show with my cousins. ☐

They seen what my dog looks like. ☐

I sat in the kitchen and done my homework. ☐

1 mark

**2** Which **word class** is the underlined word in the sentence below?

Gary's <u>brown</u> jacket looks really smart.

Tick **one**.

conjunction ☐

adverb ☐

verb ☐

adjective ☐

1 mark

**3** Which two sentences contain a **preposition**?

Tick **two**.

She walked really slowly. ☐

The rabbit munched its carrot happily. ☐

He ran around the sports field. ☐

The elderly lady walked past the window. ☐

1 mark

**4** Tick the option that shows how the underlined words in the sentence below are used.

Later in the afternoon, we played rounders.

Tick **one**.

as a main clause ☐

as a fronted adverbial ☐

as a subordinate clause ☐

as a noun phrase ☐

1 mark

**5** Replace the underlined word or words in each sentence with the correct **pronoun**.

When Joe got a pet hamster, Joe was thrilled.

[ ]

The hamster had a large cage and Joe put him in the cage.

[ ]

1 mark

**6** Tick **two** boxes to show the correct places for **inverted commas** in the sentence below.

Tick **two**.

☐ ☐         ☐    ☐
↓ ↓         ↓    ↓
Look at this beetle! It's got shiny wings, said Alex.

1 mark

**7** Tick the correct option to complete the sentence below.

_____ Shaun got ready for work.

Tick **one**.

| | |
|---|---|
| Before the sun came, up | ☐ |
| Before, the sun came up | ☐ |
| Before the sun, came up | ☐ |
| Before the sun came up, | ☐ |

1 mark

**8** Circle the correct **verb form** in each underlined pair to complete the sentences below.

Tyrone and Jax was / were waiting for Rudy to get ready.

At the park, there was / were so many fun things to do.

The teacher thought it was / were a good challenge.

1 mark

**9** Tick the option that shows how the underlined words in the sentence below are used.

Jenny has <u>a large, thin, stripy kite</u> at home.

Tick **one**.

as a fronted adverbial ☐

as a noun phrase ☐

as a subordinate clause ☐

as a main clause ☐

1 mark

**10** Replace the underlined word or words in each sentence with the correct **possessive pronoun**.

That book belongs to <u>me</u>. That book is _____.

The cake is for both of <u>us</u>. The cake is _____.

These pens belong to <u>my sister</u>. These pens are _____.

1 mark

**11** Underline the **fronted adverbial** in the sentence below.

On Friday, Denisa is playing in a netball match.

1 mark

**12** Tick the option that shows how the underlined words in the sentence below are used.

We walked past the spooky house <u>on the hill</u>.

                                          Tick **one**.

- as a main clause ☐
- as a relative clause ☐
- as a preposition phrase ☐
- as a fronted adverbial ☐

*1 mark*

**13** Add **inverted commas** to the sentence below to show what Eric is saying.

Eric yelled, Wait! I'm right behind you. Let me catch up.

*1 mark*

**14** Circle all the **pronouns** in the sentence below.

Our neighbour lets us play in her beautiful garden while she chats with my mum.

*1 mark*

**15** Which sentence is punctuated correctly?

                                          Tick **one**.

- Lately, we've been swimming every morning. ☐
- Lately we've, been swimming every morning. ☐
- Lately we've been, swimming every morning. ☐
- Lately we've been swimming, every morning. ☐

*1 mark*

**16** Which sentence is grammatically correct?

Tick **one**.

Mary done the painting. ☐

The class done its best. ☐

I have done all the hard work. ☐

Chris knows what he done wrong. ☐

1 mark

**17** Add **inverted commas** to the sentence below to show what Bethan is saying.

Bethan asked, Do you want to go to the park?

1 mark

**18** Insert a **comma** after the fronted adverbial in the sentence below.

Next weekend we are going to visit my relatives.

1 mark

**19** Circle the **adjective** in the sentence below.

I love looking at the huge dinosaur skeletons at the museum.

1 mark

**20** What is the grammatical term for the underlined part of the sentence?

<u>Without warning,</u> a flock of birds shot up into the sky.

Tick **one**.

| | |
|---|---|
| main clause | ☐ |
| noun phrase | ☐ |
| subordinate clause | ☐ |
| fronted adverbial | ☐ |

1 mark

**21** Complete the sentence below with a **preposition phrase**.

The children _____ were talking very loudly.

1 mark

**22** Circle the **possessive pronoun** in the sentence below.

They thought the weather would stay sunny so they left their umbrellas at home.

1 mark

**23** Tick all the sentences that contain a **preposition**.

| | |
|---|---|
| The beehive is full of busy bees. | ☐ |
| The man across the road is elderly. | ☐ |
| The elephant looks tired. | ☐ |
| The cat beneath the table is hiding. | ☐ |

1 mark

**24** Which option uses **inverted commas** correctly?

Tick **one**.

"Lewis said, Do you like my new notepad?" ☐

Lewis said, "Do you like my new notepad?" ☐

Lewis said, "Do you like my new notepad"? ☐

Lewis said, Do you like my "new notepad"? ☐

1 mark

**25** Which sentence is written in **Standard English**?

Tick **one**.

Some visitors come to our school yesterday. ☐

My teacher were waiting to greet them. ☐

Class 3 done them a song. ☐

I thought the visitors were interesting. ☐

1 mark

**26** Circle all the **pronouns** in the sentence below.

Cassie built a den in her back garden using Grandpa's wood and his tools.

1 mark

**27** Insert a **comma** after the fronted adverbial in the sentence below.

Every now and then Mum takes us to the market.

1 mark

**28** Write an appropriate **adjective** in the box to expand the noun phrase in the sentence.

We played under the ☐ tree.

1 mark

**29** Add **inverted commas** to the sentence below to show what Nora is saying.

You should go to bed and get some sleep, Nora said.

1 mark

**30** Replace the underlined word or words in each sentence with the correct **pronoun**.

Tom entered a competition and Tom won!

☐

Tom's story was interesting and Tom's story was funny.

☐

1 mark

Total: _____ /30

# Spring Half Term 2

**1** Which sentence is in the **present perfect** tense?

Tick **one**.

Seb was playing the piano. ☐

Seb is playing the piano. ☐

Seb played the piano. ☐

Seb has played the piano. ☐

1 mark

**2** Tick **one** box in each row to show whether the underlined noun is **singular** or **plural**.

| Sentence | Singular | Plural |
| --- | --- | --- |
| <u>Amy's</u> pencil has snapped. | | |
| Are the <u>boys'</u> torches new? | | |
| The <u>bird's</u> nest is empty. | | |

2 marks

**3** Underline the **noun phrase** in the sentence below.

I pulled on my warm fluffy socks.

1 mark

**4** Tick all the sentences that contain a **preposition**.

Tick **one**.

The red car is behind the blue bus. ☐

John collected his coat and left. ☐

My house is beside the park. ☐

Tara lives in a flat above a shop. ☐

1 mark

**5** Replace the underlined word or words in each sentence with the correct **pronoun**.

Carl rode his bike too quickly down the hill and <u>Carl</u> fell off.

[ ]

Carl grazed <u>Carl's</u> knee and scratched <u>Carl's</u> bike.

[ ]   [ ]

1 mark

**6** Which option uses **inverted commas** correctly?

Tick **one**.

Deb asked, "What time is it?" ☐

"Deb asked What time is it?" ☐

Deb asked, "What time is it"? ☐

Deb asked, "What time" is it? ☐

1 mark

**7** Circle the word in the passage that contains an **apostrophe** for **possession**.

Nik couldn't find her grandmother's cookie cutter.

It wasn't in the utensil drawer.

1 mark

**8** Which **tense** is used in the sentence below?

Darcey has written an adventure story for the annual writing competition.

Tick **one**.

| | |
|---|---|
| simple past | ☐ |
| present perfect | ☐ |
| past progressive | ☐ |
| present progressive | ☐ |

1 mark

**9** Tick all the sentences that show **plural possession**.

| | |
|---|---|
| The children's books are on the shelf. | ☐ |
| Both babies' blankets are blue and yellow. | ☐ |
| The snake's skin was shedding. | ☐ |
| Alan's tooth had been aching all day. | ☐ |

1 mark

**10** Tick the option that shows how the underlined words in the sentence below are used.

Jen wore her red flowery jacket yesterday.

Tick **one**.

as a fronted adverbial ☐

as a noun phrase ☐

as a subordinate clause ☐

as a main clause ☐

1 mark

**11** Tick the option that shows how the underlined words in the sentence below are used.

The family drove past the postbox down the road.

Tick **one**.

as a main clause ☐

as a relative clause ☐

as a preposition phrase ☐

as a fronted adverbial ☐

1 mark

**12** Which sentence uses an **apostrophe** correctly?

Tick **one**.

Andys' day was very busy. ☐

The clocks' minute hand was slow. ☐

Mondays' weather was rainy. ☐

The women's group meets at 3pm. ☐

1 mark

**13** Replace the underlined word or words in each sentence with the correct **possessive pronoun**.

That game belongs to them. That game is _____.

This watch belongs to my brother. This watch is _____.

The letter is for you. The letter is _____.

1 mark

**14** Which option completes the sentence in the **present perfect**?

Beth _____ her book.

Tick **one**.

| | |
|---|---|
| was finishing | ☐ |
| has finished | ☐ |
| finishes | ☐ |
| had finished | ☐ |

1 mark

**15** Tick **one** box in each row to show whether the sentence is written in the **present perfect** or the **simple past**.

| Sentence | Present perfect | Simple past |
|---|---|---|
| Fasil slept all day. | | |
| Joe has felt unwell today. | | |
| The tiger prowled around the lagoon. | | |

2 marks

**16** Tick all the sentences that show **plural possession**.

The athletes' bus arrived. ☐

The superhero's cape was too long. ☐

My friends' parents are here too. ☐

The farmers' meeting is on Monday. ☐

1 mark

**17** Circle the word in the passage that contains an **apostrophe** for **possession**.

I haven't tidied my room yet. I've been busy picking up my sister's toys.

1 mark

**18** Tick **one** box in each row to show whether the underlined word is an **adjective** or a **noun**.

| Sentence | Adjective | Noun |
| --- | --- | --- |
| We ate some banana ice cream. | | |
| I wanted to buy a red top. | | |
| Then I saw a beautiful bag. | | |

2 marks

**19** Add **inverted commas** to the sentence below to show what Simon is saying.

Simon shouted, Quick! Come here and look at this.

1 mark

**20** Tick all the sentences that contain a **preposition**.

That cake looks delicious. ☐

The submarine disappeared beneath the surface. ☐

The school across the road is shut. ☐

I bumped my elbow and now it hurts. ☐

1 mark

**21** Circle all the **pronouns** in the passage below.

Isaac put his trainers on and went to find his friends. They were at Lenny's house.

1 mark

**22** Circle the **possessive pronoun** in the sentence below.

I thought this pen was yours but it belongs to Marnie.

1 mark

**23** Complete the sentence below with a **preposition phrase**.

We went to the shop _____.

1 mark

**24** Write an appropriate **noun** in the box to expand the noun phrase in the sentence.

I put it away in the [ ] box.

1 mark

Year 4: Spring Half Term Test 2

**25** Tick **one** box in each row to show whether the underlined noun is **singular** or **plural**.

| Sentence | Singular | Plural |
|---|---|---|
| The donkeys' field is next to the farmhouse. | | |
| The tailor's scissors are sharp. | | |
| The mechanics' garage is busy. | | |

2 marks

**26** Explain how the position of the apostrophe changes the meaning of the second sentence.

1) The bat's wings flapped quickly.

2) The bats' wings flapped quickly.

_____

_____

1 mark

Total: _____/30

# Summer Half Term 1

**1** Which sentence is written in **Standard English**?

Tick **one**.

I saw a huge hot air balloon landing. ☐

I been to the animal sanctuary. ☐

We seen what the moon looks like tonight. ☐

They done their homework already. ☐

1 mark

**2** Circle the **adjective** in the sentence below.

Mum   bought   me   a   black   school   bag   and   a   coat.

1 mark

**3** Tick the option that shows how the underlined words in the sentence below are used.

Laura planted the small carrot seeds in her allotment.

Tick **one**.

as a fronted adverbial ☐

as a noun phrase ☐

as a subordinate clause ☐

as a main clause ☐

1 mark

**4** Tick the option that shows how the underlined words in the sentence below are used.

<u>When we woke up,</u> it was time to get ready and go.

Tick **one**.

as a main clause ☐

as a fronted adverbial ☐

as a subordinate clause ☐

as a noun phrase ☐

1 mark

**5** Tick two boxes to show the correct places for **inverted commas** in the sentence below.

Tick **two**.

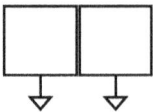       ☐                    ☐

I can't wait to see all the different aircraft, said Cam.

1 mark

**6** Insert a **comma** after the fronted adverbial in the sentence below.

Before dinner we are going to play a game.

1 mark

**7** Circle the correct **verb form** in each underlined pair to complete the sentences below.

Ahmed was / were waiting for a phone call.

At the party, there was / were lots of children.

Kitty knew she was / were a good runner.

1 mark

**8** Which **word class** are the underlined words in the sentence below?

Tara's long, neat plait kept her hair out of the way.

Tick **one**.

| | |
|---|---|
| conjunctions | ☐ |
| adverbs | ☐ |
| verbs | ☐ |
| adjectives | ☐ |

1 mark

**9** Tick the correct option to complete the sentence below.

_____ Leo rehearsed for the play.

Tick **one**.

| | |
|---|---|
| Every, day after, school | ☐ |
| Every, day after school | ☐ |
| Every day after, school | ☐ |
| Every day after school, | ☐ |

1 mark

**10** Tick **one** box in each row to show whether the underlined word is an **adjective** or a **noun**.

| Sentence | Adjective | Noun |
|---|---|---|
| We sat in the school garden. | | |
| I ate my cheese sandwich. | | |
| I drank a glass of fresh water. | | |

2 marks

**11** Add **inverted commas** to the sentence below to show what Jane is saying.

Jane whispered, Did you hear that strange noise? Listen!

1 mark

**12** Which sentence is punctuated correctly?

Tick **one**.

After the sun set we packed, up our game. ☐

After the sun set, we packed up our game. ☐

After, the sun set we packed up our game. ☐

After the sun, set we packed up our game. ☐

1 mark

**13** Underline the **noun phrase** in the sentence below.

The new yellow football is over there.

1 mark

**14** Which sentence is written in **Standard English**?

Tick **one**.

I were waiting for ages. ☐

We did lots of singing. ☐

Clint done nothing all day. ☐

I thought we was going for a walk. ☐

1 mark

**15** Underline the **fronted adverbial** in the sentence below.

On Saturday, Jack is travelling on a steam train.

1 mark

**16** Which sentence is written in **Standard English**?

Tick **one**.

I don't know what you is planning. ☐

I reckon they was spying on us. ☐

I think we did a good job on the tree house. ☐

Heena done the painting by herself. ☐

1 mark

**17** Tick one box to show which word in the sentence below is a **noun**.

Tick **one**.

My new leather shoes are really shiny.
⇧   ⇧   ⇧   ⇧
☐   ☐   ☐   ☐

1 mark

**18** Insert a **comma** after the **fronted adverbial** in the sentence below.

In a flash Ravi appeared in the doorway.

1 mark

**19** Write a **noun phrase** containing at least **three** words to complete the sentence below.
Remember to punctuate your answer correctly.

I unwrapped _____

1 mark

**20** Which sentence is grammatically correct?

Tick **one**.

She has done the hard work.          ☐

Katie done the hard work.            ☐

We all done the hard work.           ☐

Anna knows what hard work she done.  ☐

1 mark

**21** Write an appropriate **adjective** in the box to expand the noun phrase in the sentence.

I read the [ _____ ] book.

1 mark

**22** What is the grammatical term for the underlined part of the sentence below?

On a dark and stormy night, a young man walked along the street.

Tick **one**.

a main clause ☐

a noun phrase ☐

a subordinate clause ☐

a fronted adverbial ☐

1 mark

**23** What is the **word class** of the underlined word in the sentence below?

Our school uniform is red and black.

Tick **one**.

noun ☐

adverb ☐

verb ☐

adjective ☐

1 mark

**24.** Write a **noun phrase** containing at least **three** words to complete the sentence below.
Remember to punctuate your answer correctly.

I sat on _____

1 mark

**25.** Which option uses **inverted commas** correctly?

Tick **one**.

"What shall we do this weekend? asked Regan". ☐

"What shall we do this weekend"? asked Regan. ☐

What shall we do "this weekend?" asked Regan. ☐

"What shall we do this weekend?" asked Regan. ☐

1 mark

**26.** Which sentence is punctuated correctly?

Tick **one**.

As, the clock struck, twelve I fell asleep. ☐

As the clock struck, twelve I fell asleep. ☐

As the clock struck twelve, I fell asleep. ☐

As the clock, struck twelve I fell asleep. ☐

1 mark

**27** Which sentence is written in **Standard English**?

Tick **one**.

Jamal has been to watch a tennis match. ☐

Emma been playing tennis with her friends. ☐

Jamal seen some tennis champions. ☐

Emma and Jamal both done fun things. ☐

1 mark

**28** Tick the correct option to complete the sentence below.

_____, we wrote thank you letters.

Tick **one**.

The visitors were fun ☐

Visitors had gone now ☐

After the visitors left ☐

Our teacher told us ☐

1 mark

**29** Write an appropriate **adjective** in the box to expand the noun phrase in the sentence.

I used the [         ] pens.

1 mark

Total: _____/30

# Summer Half Term 2

**1** Which option completes the sentence in the **present perfect**?

Dan _____ his trumpet for three hours.

Tick **one**.

was playing ☐
has played ☐
plays ☐
had played ☐

1 mark

**2** Tick **one** box in each row to show whether the underlined noun is **singular** or **plural**.

| Sentence | Singular | Plural |
|---|---|---|
| The <u>buses'</u> depot was busy. | | |
| The <u>frogs'</u> pond is overflowing. | | |
| <u>Tilly's</u> trousers are grey. | | |

2 marks

**3** Which sentence is written in **Standard English**?

Tick **one**.

I went to the cinema with my cousin. ☐

I been to the circus with my friends. ☐

We seen what a spaceship looks like. ☐

I already done my spellings today. ☐

1 mark

**4** Tick the **adjective** in the sentence below.

Tick **one**.

The graceful stork flapped her wings as she flew away.
    ⬆    ⬆              ⬆          ⬆
    ☐    ☐              ☐          ☐

1 mark

**5** Underline the **noun phrase** in the sentence below.

The grey metal bucket is full of holes.

1 mark

**6** Tick the **preposition phrase** below.

Tick **one**.

like a rocket ☐

in a few minutes ☐

a rosy red apple ☐

on the hill ☐

1 mark

**7** Tick the option that shows how the underlined words in the sentence below are used.

Before long, the grey clouds gathered in the sky.

Tick **one**.

as a main clause ☐

as a fronted adverbial ☐

as a subordinate clause ☐

as a noun phrase ☐

1 mark

**8** Replace the underlined word or words in each sentence with the correct **pronoun**.

When Paul went to his new school, Paul was nervous.

☐

The school was big and the school was full of older pupils.

☐

1 mark

**9** Add **inverted commas** to the sentence below to show what Eve is saying.

Eve declared, I would like to be a scientist.

1 mark

**10** Write an **apostrophe** in the correct place in the sentence below.

Tanyas notebook has blue paper.

1 mark

**11** Tick one box to show where **a comma** should go in the sentence below.

Tick **one**.

Many years ago there were no mobile phones.
☐ ☐ ☐ ☐

1 mark

**12** Which sentence is in the **present perfect**?

Tick **one**.

Adam is playing basketball. ☐

Adam was playing basketball. ☐

Adam has played basketball. ☐

Adam will play basketball. ☐

1 mark

**13** Circle the correct **verb form** in each underlined pair to complete the sentences below.

Wendy is / are listening to an audio book.

Down our street, there is / are so many friendly people.

My teacher thinks it is / are a good story.

1 mark

**14** What is the **word class** of the underlined word in the sentence below?

The herd of <u>lazy</u> cows rested under the tree.

Tick **one**.

- determiner ☐
- preposition ☐
- noun ☐
- adjective ☐

1 mark

**15** What is the grammatical term for the underlined part of the sentence?

<u>His black padded winter coat with a hood</u> was at home.

Tick **one**.

- an exclamation ☐
- a main clause ☐
- a noun phrase ☐
- a command ☐

1 mark

**16** Complete the sentence with a **preposition phrase**.

The flock of birds flew _____.

1 mark

**17** Underline the **fronted adverbial** in the sentence below.

Without a sound, Todd crept downstairs and hid.

1 mark

**18** Replace the underlined word or words in each sentence with the correct **possessive pronoun**.

That game belongs to him. That game is _____.

The fruit is for both of them. The fruit is _____.

This money belongs to her. This money is _____.

*1 mark*

**19** Tick **two** boxes to show the correct places for **inverted commas** in the sentence below.

Tick **two**.

☐ ☐  ☐   ☐
↓ ↓  ↓   ↓
Where should we look first?, asked Verity.

*1 mark*

**20** Tick **one** box in each row to show whether the apostrophe has been used to show **possession** or **contraction**.

| Sentence | Possession | Contraction |
| --- | --- | --- |
| Gabriel's brother is called Eric. | | |
| Kim's not with Yasmin today. | | |
| Can we use Shyan's ideas? | | |

*2 marks*

**21** Tick the correct option to complete the sentence below.

_____ Tim ran as fast as he could.

Tick **one**.

In a state of chaos, and panic ☐

In a state of chaos and panic, ☐

In a state, of chaos and panic ☐

In a state, of chaos, and panic ☐

1 mark

**22** Which **tense** is used in the sentence below?

Nick was hoping to go and visit his cousins.

Tick **one**.

simple past ☐

simple present ☐

past progressive ☐

present progressive ☐

1 mark

**23** Tick all the sentences that show **plural possession**.

Put fresh sawdust in the gerbils' cage please. ☐

Sunil's friends' shoes were lined up by the door. ☐

The kitten's bed is my nan's old cushion. ☐

The electrician's van was full of tools. ☐

1 mark

**24** Which sentence is grammatically correct?

Tick **one**.

Steve done the ironing. ☐

George were keeping busy. ☐

We was all helping out. ☐

Isabelle did the sweeping. ☐

1 mark

**25** Tick the option that shows how the underlined words in the sentence below are used.

Daniel wants <u>a black and white baby rabbit</u> as a pet.

Tick **one**.

as a main clause ☐

as a fronted adverbial ☐

as a subordinate clause ☐

as a noun phrase ☐

1 mark

**26** Which **word class** is the underlined word in the sentence below?

Dad's <u>laptop</u> is the latest version available.

Tick **one**.

noun ☐

adverb ☐

verb ☐

adjective ☐

1 mark

**27** Which two sentences contain a **preposition**?

Tick **two**.

She lives near her workplace. ☐

The spider spun a beautiful web. ☐

We are going swimming today. ☐

The car drove through the tunnel. ☐

1 mark

**28** Insert a **comma** after the **fronted adverbial** in the sentence below.

Back at the house we warmed up and had something to eat.

1 mark

Total: _____ /30

# Mark scheme for Autumn Half Term 1

| Qu. | Requirement | Mark |
|---|---|---|
| 1<br>G1 | **Award 1 mark** for the words *an*, *a* and *the* circled. | 1m |
| 2<br>G1 | **Award 1 mark** for a tick in the second box, under *when*. | 1m |
| 3<br>G1 | **Award 2 marks** for all three boxes ticked correctly:<br>Imogen had a colourful kite. = Adjective<br>She took her kite outside. = Adverb<br>The wind swiftly lifted the kite into the sky. = Adverb<br>**Additional guidance**<br>• Award 1 mark if two boxes are ticked correctly. | 2m |
| 4<br>G1 | **Award 1 mark** for ticks next to the first, second and third sentences. | 1m |
| 5<br>G4 | **Award 1 mark** for a tick next to the first sentence: He has gone home. | 1m |
| 6<br>G5 | **Award 1 mark** for correct placement of inverted commas: Andrew squealed, "I am excited about running in the relay race." | 1m |
| 7<br>G5 | **Award 2 marks** for all three boxes ticked correctly:<br>Here are the cats' bowls. = Plural<br>I have the girl's books. = Singular<br>There are the boys' shoes. = Plural<br>**Additional guidance**<br>• Award 1 mark if two boxes are ticked correctly. | 2m |
| 8<br>G3 | **Award 1 mark** for the noun phrase *the brand new action movie* underlined. | 1m |
| 9<br>G1 | **Award 1 mark** for a tick next to the third option: Later that evening | 1m |
| 10<br>G5 | **Award 1 mark** for correct placement of inverted commas: Natasha asked, "Do you want a sandwich for your lunch today?" | 1m |
| 11<br>G5 | **Award 1 mark** for a tick next to the fourth sentence: Immediately after school, we went fishing. | 1m |
| 12<br>G1 | **Award 1 mark** for *a* (a butterfly), *a* (a spade) and *an* (an hour) written on the lines. | 1m |
| 13<br>G1 | **Award 1 mark** for the words *Once* and *since* circled. | 1m |
| 14<br>G1 | **Award 1 mark** for the word *usually* circled. | 1m |
| 15<br>G1 | **Award 1 mark** for a tick next to the second option: in | 1m |
| 16<br>G4 | **Award 1 mark** for a tick next to the third option: has read | 1m |

Year 4: Autumn Half Term Test 1 – Mark Scheme

| Qu. | Requirement | Mark |
|---|---|---|
| 17<br>G5 | **Award 1 mark** for a tick next to the first option: Grandmother asked, "Do you have a tent?" | 1m |
| 18<br>G5 | **Award 1 mark** for a tick next to the third sentence: The children's toys were scattered on the floor. | 1m |
| 19<br>G1 G3 | **Award 1 mark** for the use of any appropriate adjective, for example: *deep, cold, sparkling*. | 1m |
| 20<br>G1 | **Award 1 mark** for a tick next to the second option: as a fronted adverbial | 1m |
| 21<br>G5 | **Award 1 mark** for correct placement of inverted commas: Kira explained, "We climbed to the top of the mountain!" | 1m |
| 22<br>G1 G5 | **Award 1 mark** for a tick in the second box: As quick as a flash, the rabbit disappeared into a hole. | 1m |
| 23<br>G1 | **Award 1 mark** for all three conjunctions inserted correctly:<br>You can go outside <u>and</u> play cricket <u>or</u> basketball, <u>but</u> you mustn't go on the wet grass. | 1m |
| 24<br>G1 | **Award 1 mark** for a tick next to the second option: adverb | 1m |
| 25<br>G1 | **Award 1 mark** for the word *under* circled. | 1m |
| 26<br>G5 | **Award 1 mark** for a tick next to the fourth option: Amit asked, "Shall we have a barbecue today?" | 1m |
| 27<br>G1 | **Award 1 mark** for the use of any appropriate fronted adverbial, for example: *Later that day, In the morning, Without warning*. | 1m |
| 28<br>G5 | **Award 1 mark** for a tick next to the second option: friends' | 1m |

# Mark scheme for Autumn Half Term 2

| Qu. | Requirement | Mark |
|---|---|---|
| 1<br>G5 | **Award 1 mark** for a tick next to the first sentence: The cats' tails are long and fluffy. | 1m |
| 2<br>G1 | **Award 2 marks** for all three boxes ticked correctly:<br>We waited by the <u>oak</u> tree. = Noun<br>I saw a <u>hairy</u> spider. = Adjective<br>My mum is a <u>famous</u> artist. = Adjective<br>**Additional guidance**<br>• Award 1 mark if two boxes are ticked correctly | 2m |
| 3<br>G5 | **Award 1 mark** for ticks in the first and third boxes. | 1m |
| 4<br>G5 | **Award 2 marks** for all three boxes ticked correctly:<br>The <u>girls'</u> bus has arrived at the bus stop. = Plural<br>Did you see the <u>rocket's</u> boosters? = Singular<br><u>Val's</u> hats are in the cupboard. = Singular<br>**Additional guidance**<br>• Award 1 mark if two boxes are ticked correctly. | 2m |
| 5<br>G5 | **Award 1 mark** for a tick next to the third sentence: The foxes' den is near the old tree. | 1m |
| 6<br>G5 | **Award 1 mark** for the word *Rebecca's* circled. | 1m |
| 7<br>G1 | **Award 1 mark** for ticks in the second and third boxes. | 1m |
| 8<br>G5 | **Award 2 marks** for all three boxes ticked correctly:<br>The <u>eagle's</u> nest is high up on the rocks. = Singular<br>The <u>volcanoes'</u> craters formed many years ago. = Plural<br>The <u>boys'</u> cinema tickets are in my pocket. = Plural<br>**Additional guidance**<br>• Award 1 mark if two boxes are ticked correctly. | 2m |
| 9<br>G5 | **Award 1 mark** for ticks next to the first and third sentences. | 1m |
| 10<br>G5 | **Award 1 mark** for correct placement of inverted commas: Hikmat moaned, "I would prefer to have chips for dinner." | 1m |
| 11<br>G3 | **Award 1 mark** for the noun phrase *The blue china tea cup* underlined. | 1m |
| 12<br>G5 | **Award 1 mark** for the word *Max's* circled. | 1m |
| 13<br>G5 | **Award 1 mark** for correct placement of inverted commas: "Please wipe your shoes on the mat when you enter the house," said David. | 1m |

Year 4: Autumn Half Term Test 2 – Mark Scheme

| Qu. | Requirement | Mark |
|---|---|---|
| 14 G5 | **Award 2 marks** for all three boxes ticked correctly: <br> The <u>families'</u> cars were parked along the street. = Plural <br> The <u>parents'</u> evening is on Tuesday. = Plural <br> The <u>woman's</u> scarf is on the chair. = Singular <br> **Additional guidance** <br> • Award 1 mark if two boxes are ticked correctly. | 2m |
| 15 G5 | **Award 1 mark** for a tick next to the third sentence: My sisters' toy box has a broken lid. | 1m |
| 16 G3 | **Award 1 mark** for a tick next to the third option: a noun phrase | 1m |
| 17 G5 | **Award 1 mark** for an apostrophe after the final letter *s* in *classes*: The classes' performance was great. | 1m |
| 18 G5 | **Award 1 mark** for a tick next to the fourth option: "Shall we watch the cricket match?" asked Dev. | 1m |
| 19 G5 | **Award 1 mark** for ticks next to the second and third sentences. | 1m |
| 20 G3 | **Award 1 mark** for the noun phrase *a Young Savers bank account* underlined. | 1m |
| 21 G5 | **Award 1 mark** for a tick next to the second sentence: Giraffes' necks are very long. | 1m |
| 22 G3 | **Award 1 mark** for the use of any appropriate noun phrase containing three or more words, for example: *an old fence, a brick wall, the wall with red bricks*. | 1m |
| 23 G3 | **Award 1 mark** for a tick next to the first option: a noun phrase | 1m |
| 24 G5 | **Award 1 mark** for a response that demonstrates understanding of the plural possessive apostrophe, e.g. <br> • In the second sentence, it means there is more than one girl. <br> • In the second one, it shows plural possession. <br> • 1. One girl. 2. Two girls. <br> **Also accept** responses that demonstrate understanding without referring to the second sentence, e.g. <br> In the first sentence, there is only one girl. <br> **There are no spelling or punctuation requirements for this question.** | 1m |
| 25 G1 G3 | **Award 1 mark** for the use of any appropriate noun, for example: *clothes, toy, corner*. | 1m |
| 26 G5 | **Award 1 mark** for ticks next to the first and fourth sentences. | 1m |

# Mark scheme for Spring Half Term 1

| Qu. | Requirement | Mark |
|---|---|---|
| 1<br>G7 | **Award 1 mark** for a tick next to the first sentence: I went to the museum with my class. | 1m |
| 2<br>G1 | **Award 1 mark** for a tick next to the fourth option: adjective | 1m |
| 3<br>G1 | **Award 1 mark** for ticks next to the third and fourth sentences. | 1m |
| 4<br>G1 | **Award 1 mark** for a tick next to the second option: as a fronted adverbial | 1m |
| 5<br>G1 | **Award 1 mark** for the pronouns *he* and *it* written in the boxes. | 1m |
| 6<br>G5 | **Award 1 mark** for ticks in the first and fourth boxes: "Look at this beetle! It's got shiny wings," said Alex. | 1m |
| 7<br>G5 | **Award 1 mark** for a tick next to the fourth option: Before the sun came up, | 1m |
| 8<br>G7 | **Award 1 mark** for *were*, *were* and *was* circled.<br>• Tyrone and Jax <u>were</u> waiting for Rudy to get ready.<br>• At the park, there <u>were</u> so many fun things to do.<br>• The teacher thought it <u>was</u> a good challenge. | 1m |
| 9<br>G3 | **Award 1 mark** for a tick next to the second option: as a noun phrase. | 1m |
| 10<br>G1 | **Award 1 mark** for the words *mine*, *ours* and *hers* written on the lines.<br>• That book belongs to <u>me</u>. That book is <u>mine</u>.<br>• The cake is for both of <u>us</u>. The cake is <u>ours</u>.<br>• These pens belong to <u>my sister</u>. These pens are <u>hers</u>. | 1m |
| 11<br>G1 | **Award 1 mark** for the fronted adverbial *On Friday,* underlined. | 1m |
| 12<br>G1 | **Award 1 mark** for a tick next to the third option: as a preposition phrase | 1m |
| 13<br>G5 | **Award 1 mark** for correct placement of inverted commas: Eric yelled, "Wait! I'm right behind you. Let me catch up." | 1m |
| 14<br>G1 | **Award 1 mark** for the words *Our*, *us*, *her*, *she* and *my* circled. | 1m |
| 15<br>G5 | **Award 1 mark** for a tick next to the first sentence: Lately, we've been swimming every morning. | 1m |
| 16<br>G7 | **Award 1 mark** for a tick next to the third sentence: I have done all the hard work. | 1m |
| 17<br>G5 | **Award 1 mark** for correct placement of inverted commas: Bethan asked, "Do you want to go to the park?" | 1m |

Year 4: Spring Half Term Test 1 – Mark Scheme

| Qu. | Requirement | Mark |
|---|---|---|
| 18 G5 | **Award 1 mark** for a comma inserted after the word *weekend*. | 1m |
| 19 G1 | **Award 1 mark** for the word *huge* circled. | 1m |
| 20 G1 | **Award 1 mark** for a tick next to the fourth option: fronted adverbial | 1m |
| 21 G3 | **Award 1 mark** for the use of any appropriate preposition phrase, for example: *on the bus, at the back, in the hall*. | 1m |
| 22 G1 | **Award 1 mark** for the word *their* circled. | 1m |
| 23 G1 | **Award 1 mark** for ticks next to the second and fourth sentences. | 1m |
| 24 G5 | **Award 1 mark** for a tick next to the second option: Lewis said, "Do you like my new notepad?" | 1m |
| 25 G7 | **Award 1 mark** for a tick next to the fourth sentence: I thought the visitors were interesting. | 1m |
| 26 G1 | **Award 1 mark** for the words *her* and *his* circled. | 1m |
| 27 G1 G5 | **Award 1 mark** for a comma inserted after the word *then*. | 1m |
| 28 G1 G3 | **Award 1 mark** for the use of any appropriate adjective, for example: *enormous, old, sturdy*. | 1m |
| 29 G5 | **Award 1 mark** for correct placement of inverted commas: "You should go to bed and get some sleep," Nora said. | 1m |
| 30 G1 | **Award 1 mark** for the pronouns *he* and *it* written in the boxes. | 1m |

# Mark scheme for Spring Half Term 2

| Qu. | Requirement | Mark |
|---|---|---|
| 1<br>G4 | **Award 1 mark** for a tick next to the fourth sentence: Seb has played the piano. | 1m |
| 2<br>G5 | **Award 2 marks** for all three boxes ticked correctly:<br>Amy's pencil has snapped. = Singular<br>Are the boys' torches new? = Plural<br>The bird's nest is empty. = Singular<br>**Additional guidance**<br>• Award 1 mark if two boxes are ticked correctly. | 2m |
| 3<br>G3 | **Award 1 mark** for the noun phrase *my warm fluffy socks* underlined. | 1m |
| 4<br>G1 | **Award 1 mark** for ticks next to the first, third and fourth sentences. | 1m |
| 5<br>G1 | **Award 1 mark** for the pronouns *he*, *his* and *his* written in the boxes. | 1m |
| 6<br>G5 | **Award 1 mark** for a tick next to the first option: Deb asked, "What time is it?" | 1m |
| 7<br>G5 | **Award 1 mark** for the word *grandmother's* circled. | 1m |
| 8<br>G4 | **Award 1 mark** for a tick next to the second option: present perfect | 1m |
| 9<br>G5 | **Award 1 mark** for ticks next to the first and second sentences. | 1m |
| 10<br>G3 | **Award 1 mark** for a tick next to the second option: as a noun phrase | 1m |
| 11<br>G1 | **Award 1 mark** for a tick next to the third option: as a preposition phrase | 1m |
| 12<br>G5 | **Award 1 mark** for a tick next to the fourth sentence: The women's group meets at 3pm. | 1m |
| 13<br>G1 | **Award 1 mark** for the words *theirs*, *his*, *yours* written on the lines.<br>• That game belongs to them. That game is theirs.<br>• This watch belongs to my brother. This watch is his.<br>• The letter is for you. The letter is yours. | 1m |
| 14<br>G4 | **Award 1 mark** for a tick next to the second option: has finished | 1m |
| 15<br>G4 | **Award 2 marks** for all three boxes ticked correctly:<br>Fasil slept all day. = Simple past<br>Joe has felt unwell today. = Present perfect<br>The tiger prowled around the lagoon. = Simple past<br>**Additional guidance**<br>• Award 1 mark if two boxes are ticked correctly. | 2m |
| 16<br>G5 | **Award 1 mark** for ticks next to the first, third and fourth sentences. | 1m |

Year 4: Spring Half Term Test 2 – Mark scheme

| Qu. | Requirement | Mark |
|---|---|---|
| 17 G5 | **Award 1 mark** for the word *sister's* circled. | 1m |
| 18 G1 | **Award 2 marks** for all three boxes ticked correctly: <br><br>We ate some banana ice cream. = Noun <br>I wanted to buy a red top. = Adjective <br>Then I saw a beautiful bag. = Adjective <br><br>**Additional guidance** <br><br>• Award 1 mark if two boxes are ticked correctly. | 2m |
| 19 G5 | **Award 1 mark** for correct placement of inverted commas: Simon shouted, "Quick! Come here and look at this." | 1m |
| 20 G1 | **Award 1 mark** for ticks next to the second and third sentences. | 1m |
| 21 G1 | **Award 1 mark** for the words *his*, *his* and *They* circled. | 1m |
| 22 G1 | **Award 1 mark** for the word *yours* circled | 1m |
| 23 G3 | **Award 1 mark** for the use of any appropriate preposition phrase, for example: *on the corner, down the street*. | 1m |
| 24 G1 G3 | **Award 1 mark** for the use of any appropriate noun, for example: *toy, cardboard, puzzle, pencil*. | 1m |
| 25 G5 | **Award 2 marks** for all three boxes ticked correctly: <br><br>The donkeys' field is next to the farmhouse. = Plural <br>The tailor's scissors are sharp. = Singular <br>The mechanics' garage is busy. = Plural <br><br>**Additional guidance** <br><br>• Award 1 mark if two boxes are ticked correctly. | 2m |
| 26 G5 | **Award 1 mark** for a response that demonstrates understanding of the plural possessive apostrophe, e.g. <br><br>• In the second sentence, it means there is more than one bat. <br>• In the second one, it shows plural possession. <br>• 1. One bat. 2. Two bats. <br><br>**Also accept** responses that demonstrate understanding without referring to the second sentence, e.g. <br><br>In the first sentence, there is only one bat. <br><br>**There are no spelling or punctuation requirements for this question.** | 1m |

# Mark scheme for Summer Half Term 1

| Qu. | Requirement | Mark |
|---|---|---|
| 1<br>G7 | **Award 1 mark** for a tick next to the first sentence: I saw a huge hot air balloon landing. | 1m |
| 2<br>G1 | **Award 1 mark** for the word *black* circled. | 1m |
| 3<br>G3 | **Award 1 mark** for a tick next to the second option: as a noun phrase | 1m |
| 4<br>G1 | **Award 1 mark** for a tick next to the second option: as a fronted adverbial | 1m |
| 5<br>G5 | **Award 1 mark** for ticks in the first and fourth boxes. | 1m |
| 6<br>G1 G5 | **Award 1 mark** for a comma after the word *dinner*: Before dinner, we are going to play a game. | 1m |
| 7<br>G7 | **Award 1 mark** for circles around *was*, *were* and *was*:<br>• Ahmed was waiting for a phone call.<br>• At the party, there were lots of children.<br>• Kitty knew she was a good runner. | 1m |
| 8<br>G1 | **Award 1 mark** for a tick next to the fourth option: adjectives | 1m |
| 9<br>G5 | **Award 1 mark** for a tick next to the fourth option: Every day after school, | 1m |
| 10<br>G1 | **Award 2 marks** for all three boxes ticked correctly:<br>We sat in the school garden. = Noun<br>I ate my cheese sandwich. = Noun<br>I drank a glass of fresh water. = Adjective<br>**Additional guidance**<br>• Award 1 mark if two boxes are ticked correctly. | 2m |
| 11<br>G5 | **Award 1 mark** for correct placement of inverted commas: Jane whispered, "Did you hear that strange noise? Listen!" | 1m |
| 12<br>G5 | **Award 1 mark** for a tick next to the second sentence: After the sun set, we packed up our game. | 1m |
| 13<br>G3 | **Award 1 mark** for the noun phrase *The new yellow football,* underlined. | 1m |
| 14<br>G7 | **Award 1 mark** for a tick next to the second sentence: We did lots of singing. | 1m |
| 15<br>G1 | **Award 1 mark** for the fronted adverbial *On Saturday,* underlined. | 1m |
| 16<br>G7 | **Award 1 mark** for a tick next to the third sentence: I think we did a good job on the tree house. | 1m |
| 17<br>G1 | **Award 1 mark** for a tick in the third box. | 1m |

Year 4: Summer Half Term Test 1 – Mark scheme

| Qu. | Requirement | Mark |
|---|---|---|
| 18 G1 G5 | **Award 1 mark** for a comma after the word *flash*: In a flash, Ravi appeared in the doorway. | 1m |
| 19 G3 | **Award 1 mark** for the use of any appropriate noun phrase, for example: *the delicate present, a huge colourful gift*. | 1m |
| 20 G7 | **Award 1 mark** for a tick next to the first sentence: She has done the hard work. | 1m |
| 21 G1 G3 | **Award 1 mark** for the use of any appropriate adjective, for example: *exciting, red, large, old*. | 1m |
| 22 G1 | **Award 1 mark** for a tick next to the fourth option: a fronted adverbial | 1m |
| 23 G1 | **Award 1 mark** for a tick next to the first option: noun | 1m |
| 24 G3 | **Award 1 mark** for the use of any appropriate noun phrase, for example: *the bouncy chair, the hard floor*. | 1m |
| 25 G5 | **Award 1 mark** for a tick next to the fourth option: '"What shall we do this weekend?" asked Regan. | 1m |
| 26 G5 | **Award 1 mark** for a tick next to the third sentence: As the clock struck twelve, I fell asleep. | 1m |
| 27 G7 | **Award 1 mark** for a tick next to the first sentence: Jamal has been to watch a tennis match. | 1m |
| 28 G1 | **Award 1 mark** for a tick next to the third option: After the visitors left | 1m |
| 29 G1 G3 | **Award 1 mark** for the use of any appropriate adjective, for example: *fluorescent, felt, colourful*. | 1m |

# Mark scheme for Summer Half Term 2

| Qu. | Requirement | Mark |
|---|---|---|
| 1<br>G4 | **Award 1 mark** for a tick next to the second option: has played | 1m |
| 2<br>G5 | **Award 2 marks** for all three boxes ticked correctly:<br>The buses' depot was busy. = Plural<br>The frogs' pond is overflowing. = Plural<br>Tilly's trousers are grey. = Singular<br>**Additional guidance**<br>• Award 1 mark if two boxes are ticked correctly. | 2m |
| 3<br>G7 | **Award 1 mark** for a tick next to the first sentence: I went to the cinema with my cousins. | 1m |
| 4<br>G3 | **Award 1 mark** for a tick in the first box: graceful | 1m |
| 5<br>G3 | **Award 1 mark** for the noun phrase *The grey metal bucket* underlined. | 1m |
| 6<br>G1 | **Award 1 mark** for a tick next to the fourth option: on the hill | 1m |
| 7<br>G1 | **Award 1 mark** for a tick next to the second option: as a fronted adverbial | 1m |
| 8<br>G1 | **Award 1 mark** for the pronouns *he* and *it* written in the boxes. | 1m |
| 9<br>G5 | **Award 1 mark** for correct placement of inverted commas: Eve declared, "I would like to be a scientist." | 1m |
| 10<br>G5 | **Award 1 mark** for an apostrophe after the second letter *a* in *Tanyas*: Tanya's notebook has blue paper. | 1m |
| 11<br>G5 | **Award 1 mark** for a tick in the second box. | 1m |
| 12<br>G4 | **Award 1 mark** for a tick next to the third sentence: Adam has played basketball. | 1m |
| 13<br>G4 | **Award 1 mark** for a circles around *is*, *are* and *is*:<br>• Wendy is listening to an audio book.<br>• Down our street, there are so many friendly people.<br>• My teacher thinks it is a good story. | 1m |
| 14<br>G1 | **Award 1 mark** for a tick next to the fourth option: adjective | 1m |
| 15<br>G3 | **Award 1 mark** for a tick next to the third option: a noun phrase | 1m |
| 16<br>G3 | **Award 1 mark** for the use of any appropriate preposition phrase, for example: *over the pond, past the cloud, under the bridge.* | 1m |
| 17<br>G1 | **Award 1 mark** for the fronted adverbial *Without a sound,* underlined. | 1m |

Year 4: Summer Half Term Test 2 – Mark scheme

| Qu. | Requirement | Mark |
|---|---|---|
| 18 G1 | **Award 1 mark** for the words *his*, *theirs* and *hers* written on the lines:<br>• That game belongs to him. That game is his.<br>• The fruit is for both of them. The fruit is theirs.<br>• This money belongs to her. This money is hers. | 1m |
| 19 G5 | **Award 1 mark** for ticks in the first and fourth boxes. | 1m |
| 20 G5 | **Award 2 marks** for all three boxes ticked correctly:<br>Gabriel's brother is called Eric. = Possession<br>Kim's not with Yasmin today. = Contraction<br>Can we use Shyan's ideas? = Possession<br>**Additional guidance**<br>• Award 1 mark if two boxes are ticked correctly. | 2m |
| 21 G5 | **Award 1 mark** for a tick next to the second option: In a state of chaos and panic, | 1m |
| 22 G4 | **Award 1 mark** for a tick next to the third option: past progressive | 1m |
| 23 G5 | **Award 1 mark** for ticks next to the first and second sentences. | 1m |
| 24 G7 | **Award 1 mark** for a tick next to the fourth sentence: Isabelle did the sweeping. | 1m |
| 25 G3 | **Award 1 mark** for a tick next to the fourth option: as a noun phrase | 1m |
| 26 G1 | **Award 1 mark** for a tick next to the first option: noun | 1m |
| 27 G1 | **Award 1 mark** for ticks next to the first and fourth sentences. | 1m |
| 28 G1 G5 | **Award 1 mark** for a comma inserted after the word *house*: Back at the house, we warmed up and had something to eat. | 1m |

Name:          Class:

## Year 4 Grammar, Punctuation and Vocabulary Record Sheet

| Tests | Mark | Total marks | Key skills to target |
|---|---|---|---|
| Autumn Half Term Test 1 | | | |
| Autumn Half Term Test 2 | | | |
| Spring Half Term Test 1 | | | |
| Spring Half Term Test 2 | | | |
| Summer Half Term Test 1 | | | |
| Summer Half Term Test 2 | | | |

www.ingramcontent.com/pod-product-compliance
Lightning Source LLC
Chambersburg PA
CBHW080605010526
44109CB00052B/2351